Silly Depressed

Musings on Our Mental Illness

by Kristin Hooker

STRANGE GOOSE

Silly Depressed
Copyright © 2022 by Kristin Hooker.

All rights reserved. Printed in the United States of America. No part of this book may be used or reproduced in any manner whatsoever without written permission except in the case of brief quotations em- bodied in critical articles or reviews.
This book is a work of fiction. Names, characters, businesses, organiza- tions, places, events and incidents either are the product of the author's imagination or are used fictitiously. Any resemblance to actual persons, living or dead, events, or locales is entirely coincidental.

For information contact jonathan@strangegoose.com

Paperback ISBN: 978-1-7364426-5-4
Ebook ISBN: 978-1-7364426-6-1
First Edition: March 2022

INTRODUCTION	5
INTRODUCTION 2	9
DEPRESSION IN YOUR BONES	13
I WISH I WASN'T CRYING ALSO	19
TOO SENSITIVE	27
CHILDHOOD DEPRESSION	29
VENLAFAXINE	35
UNWANTED THOUGHTS	43
THE GIGGLES	51
A REASON TO BE DEPRESSED COMES ALONG	55
AM I DEPRESSED OR AM I JUST A MORBID WEIRDO?	59
BED	63
IDGAF	67
ADVICE	71
NOTHING IS FUN	75
YOU ARE AN ALIEN PRETENDING TO BE HUMAN	79
A METAPHOR WITH SWIMMING	83
ALL THE TREATMENTS!	85
TRANSCRANIAL MAGNETIC STIMULATION	91
THE WORLD DOESN'T END TOMORROW	97
MY STUPID HOPE	103

INTRODUCTION

This is a book for goofballs who are depressed or who have been depressed before and maybe that depression became part of your personality, e.g. "The depression guy."

Perhaps you keep your depression and goofballs a secret because you want to appear professional. Maybe you wear a fleece

vest to work, sit down at a computer, and think *My God, why am I doing this? Nothing matters. Oh no, here comes someone, smile.* "Hey, Scott!" *Think of something normal to say,* "How's it do- going?" *How's it "do going?" Whatever, it doesn't matter if he thinks I'm a dumbass. We're all gonna die.*

The mundanities of life seem absurd when you're depressed. You might be asking yourself *Why am I sticking around for this? What even **is** this?*

If you believe in God, you might think that He has some kind of mission for you and ending your life is never part of the mission. No, you're going to have to wait until you are struck by a falling icicle off a skyscraper or something.

If you don't believe in God or an afterlife, then you must believe that this life is all we get- eighty years or so, out of the billions of years that this planet has been around. Such a short time; you might as well push through to the end, whether it's a plain old death or the moon exploding.

Honestly, I don't know. No one does. I'm a person of faith, but I still don't know why God decided to do all of this stuff, or why He allows me to get depressed over and over. What's the point?

So let's stop asking big questions that we can't answer and instead just have a chat about our vast internal emptiness!

All the disclaimers: (Skip this part if you don't like disclaimers, obviously.)

-The stuff in this book is mostly going to be about "depressed for no reason depression." I do not have loads of trauma in my life and I'm mostly writing about my own personal experience here. It's not narcissistic, it's memoiristic.

-I am not any kind of professional. I have a Master's Degree in Library Science- a degree which I used only slightly longer than it took me to earn it and fifteen years later, I still haven't paid off my student debt. This book is simply my thoughts about depression, both silly and poignant. I hope to encourage, but that may not mean that you personally will feel encouraged.

-My words and thoughts might be unrelatable, but my experience is valid. Your experience is valid. I apologize if you don't find my thoughts relatable. That's probably disappointing. If you are in a different place than I have been, I encourage you to find an outlet to share your thoughts and frustrations. If you don't connect with me, I hope you are able to find and connect with someone.

-I am bad at drawing and that amuses me. You may not be amused. I am not sorry about this. If you want to check out a book with good art, perhaps try Blexbolex?

-I am privileged. See Introduction Part Two.

-If you didn't like my disclaimers because you think disclaimers are for oversensitive folks, well, again, you should have skipped this section, obviously. That's on you.

INTRODUCTION TWO

Acknowledging Issues of Equity

Trigger Warning: *If you are the victim of inequity, this might be triggering for you.*

I've been struggling to know exactly what to say about privilege. In the US, equity is a massive struggle for marginalized and/or impoverished people. Even people who aren't technically impoverished struggle to provide for all of their needs.

Here is what I want to say about privilege or lack thereof:

EVERYONE DESERVES TO HAVE THEIR DEPRESSION TREATED.

Who deserves to have their depression treated?
BIPOC
Poor people
LGBTQ
Prison inmates
Children
Jerks that you don't like
Older adults
Victims
Survivors
Refugees and Immigrants
Karens[1]
Unhoused people
The people who, at one time, told you to "pull yourself up by your bootstraps"
The people who told you to "snap out of it"
You

---

[1] In US slang, a Karen is a white woman who calls the police on people. Then the police show up and she insists she was the victim of something while sipping a to-go cup of Diet Coke. Severely lacking in empathy. Treats people in the service industry poorly. Probably sports a bad haircut[11].

[11] I had this haircut in like, 1997 and, at the time, it was completely punk. I swear. (You'll see for yourself soon enough, if you keep reading.) I don't know why it was adopted by Karen types in the early 2000s.

I personally believe everyone on that list deserves access to mental health care. If they're a jerk, maybe they'd be less of a jerk if they weren't so sad all the time.

In the US, we live in a system that does not support this ideology.

Am I, the author, a Karen?! Am I privileged? These are questions you may and should be asking of me. In my humble opinion, the moment a white woman believes she is above being a Karen is the moment she is most likely to become one. So am I a Karen? My best answer is that I'm always trying not to be.

As for privilege, the closest I've come to lack of access to care was when I went into debt over getting some cavities filled back when I was single and living paycheck to paycheck. So basically, never.

I grew up in a middle-class white home. Today I live in a middle-class white home. I've always had access. And I want EVERYONE to have the access that I have.

Depression is not a contest. Everyone should be able to get it treated, no matter how minor or severe it is and no matter how privileged or underprivileged they are.

We don't just want bread. We want Prozac too.

KRISTIN HOOKER

ONE

Depression In Your Bones

A sucking vacuous hole in my chest.

A cloud of cotton balls packed around my perception of reality.

Like I

need to run away from wherever I am.

Like cold churning in my bowels.

A perpetual unnerving feeling that a person is in their car driving towards my location just so they can yell at me.

Emptiness. No personality. No feelings. Just empty.

Draw a picture of how depression or anxiety makes your body feel. Is there a weight on your shoulders? Does your hair thin? Do you get tummy troubles? Feel free to add tasteful nudity.

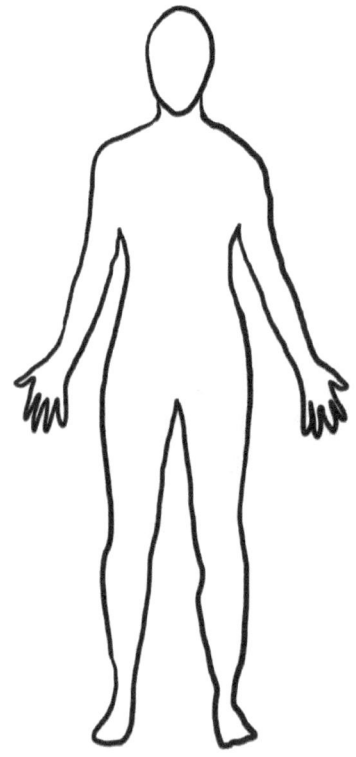

Depression makes my body feel tired. One day I was lying in a pile of laundry that I had the energy to fold, but not put away. My husband looked at me with utmost compassion and told me that maybe I should try CrossFit. This made me laugh. Has someone ever told you that exercise was good for depression? At some points in your bout of depression, perhaps you are able to get yourself to exercise. At other points, it's impossible because you can't even make yourself care about getting better and your body isn't capable of doing... whatever it is they do at CrossFit. I don't even want to know and CrossFit jokes are stale as hell.

SILLY DEPRESSED

Since exercising our bodies makes us less depressed, circle the exercises you might like to try next time you are having a dark night of the soul, if you are able.

Walking
Jogging
Roller blading
Practicing barrel rolls out of a moving vehicle
Yoga
Hot yoga
Yoga, but only the poses that involve lying down
Hiking
Snowshoeing
Buying an expensive piece of workout equipment
Rigorously dusting the workout equipment you bought the last time you were depressed
Swimming
Thigh Master
Squeezing your fists to make the bad thoughts go away
Other

Lately, I haven't been too depressed, but I started roller skating anyway. Unfortunately, if I roll into the smallest pebble or nutshell I wreck myself, so the only safe place I can skate is on my front porch. Back and forth I skate with full safety gear on and skates that look like they were meant for a 12 year old. I'm trying to learn to spin in a circle. I'm doing it now because I know the next time I'm depressed, I won't be motivated to learn to spin. I think it will be funny to take a video of myself spinning and crying.

I once took a mental health bike ride and cried while riding. It wasn't funny at the time, but in hindsight, it's pretty goofy.

If my body wants to cry, there's not much I can do to stop it. Have you ever cried in public? Is it possible for you to look back and laugh about it?

There were times when I was comforted by total strangers. It's odd- I both appreciate the kindness, but also want strangers to pretend that my crying isn't happening. Usually if someone acknowledges my crying, it makes me cry even harder.

Speaking of crying...

TWO

I Wish I Wasn't Crying Also

Yesterday I was feeling bad. I had fallen while roller skating and injured an ankle and my coccyx. I was sitting on the couch with an inflatable donut under my ass and a bandage around one ankle. I was also having an eczema flare up, a yeast infection on my face, withdrawal symptoms from quitting an

antidepressant, as well as side effects from starting a new antidepressant, some ADHD problems, and generally feeling like I needed a win.

In the midst of this, I was watching videos on a social media app and came across one where someone was talking about how people use tears to manipulate others.

Is that what people think when I cry? That I'm trying to draw sympathy?

Believe me, I also wish I wasn't crying.

When stress has mounted up and then the final straw is laid upon my back, a lump forms in my throat. I strain my eyes to hold back tears. *Oh shoot, did people think that look of strain was me trying to work up some tears?* Because, believe me, I also wish I wasn't crying.

When my neighbor insanely tried to shake me down for electric bill money for his house and he was blocking me from getting to my car for work and I didn't know what to do and I started crying and he immediately said "This is why I can't talk to you, you just start crying," even though I had never had any interaction with him like this before- Did he think I was crying on purpose?

We very much wished I wasn't crying.

And when my front house landlady yelled at me for having about five people over to the back house and it wasn't even 9 PM and she called it a "party"... did she think I squoze those tears out on purpose? She also said "This is why I can't talk to you, you just start crying," even though nothing like that had ever happened before either!

And that one time I was at the Night Light Lounge and my friend Brette told me a funny story that was *so* funny I laughed a little too hard and it made me start crying about an unrelated backlog of stress- Surely my sweet friend didn't think I was pleased with myself. Did she?

Now let me set the stage for the most humiliating time I cried in public. I was in grad school and was having serious mental illness issues. I was constantly having panic attacks. I rapidly lost about 20 lbs and I was generally a disorganized mess who struggled to read because my brain was so fuzzy. I struggled to know who my friends were. Maybe all those people around me were just friends with my bestie and *that* was the only reason I was invited to any place. Because I was attached to her hip, not because *I* was wanted. After all, being friends with the weird, awkward, depressed girl couldn't have been appealing to college students who were mostly trying to have fun. I wondered if I was crazy. I wondered if anyone would visit me if I was in the hospital. I wondered what the hell I was doing with my life.

On top of my mental woes, I also had IBS and was so neurotic about it that I once took diarrhea medicine and constipation medicine on the same day.

That's what was already happening in my body and mind when the last straw came- I had to meet with a professor because I failed a paper that threatened my ability to pass the class. She wasn't terribly kind or encouraging about it, which I didn't really expect from a graduate school professor, but it's what I would have preferred and needed in that moment. I started crying because, to me, failing a class or failing out of grad school or leaving grad school to work on my mental health would make me a loser- a sentiment I no longer hold true, but in that moment I basically felt like my life was on the verge of being over. I cried UNCONTROLLABLY in her office. I. Could. Not. Stop. Here's where it gets rich- she complained that I was oversharing, but in the same meeting told *me* that her hypothyroidism was making her pubic hair fall out.

I left her office still crying and headed for a large women's restroom so I could hide in a stall and regain my composure. I walked into the bathroom and there was a fucking line. A line containing other women from my same grad program, all trying to decide if they should comfort me or build an invisible bathroom stall around me with their minds.

I received one hug and a "yeah, that professor is tough."

At the present, I just started crying right here, right now. I shit you not. Even remembering crying makes me cry.

Just to resolve that story, I passed the class and passed grad school with a degree that said I was capable of cataloging library books and fielding questions about when our copy of "The Hills Have Eyes" would return.

Anyway, a few days ago, like I said, I was sitting on my couch with a crusty face and my ass on a donut googling "How to not cry" because, damn it, I'm almost 40 years old and I'm going to beat this thing.

Don't cry

1. Tip head back
2. Blink rapidly
3. Actually, don't blink
4. Cry 10 minutes ago instead
5. Deep breaths
6. Cause yourself a distracting amount of physical pain, but not so much that it makes you cry.

My husband found me there, looked over my shoulder and said "That's the saddest thing I've ever seen anyone google."

I burst into tears. I even tried to use some of the methods I had just read about, like tipping my head back to let gravity shove the tears back into my face. It didn't work.

And then I had a great big moment of feeling sorry for myself which my husband patiently indulged.

"I just need something good to happen (waaaaaaa) and when I put altruism out into the world, I'm not (hiccup) doing it (heaving breaths) to get something in return. But it would be ni-yi-yice. I just need a win! I need something good to happen to me!"

At this point I needed to backpedal to let him know that I appreciate that he works so I can pursue my dream of being a writer who at least makes enough money to not feel like a total freeloader. And I'm grateful for our wonderful son and wonderful house, blah blah blah. I already acknowledged my privilege in the introduction; it's just hard to have that perspective when you're having a bad moment.

"But I want something good to happen in my careeeeeeeeeeer! Why does my book only have five reviews? I review *my* friends' books. I went to *their* concerts before we all had kids. I give to *their* charities, I go to *their* birthday drinks. This is the first time I've ever asked for anythiiiiiiiing."

But I wasn't really crying about my career. Or my friends and family not reviewing my book, "Idiots and Robots." (TBH, it's very niche humor.)

The crying was about the struggle of mental illness being this invisible bale of hay on my back and sometimes a sentimental commercial or stubbed toe or a stranger calling me a "bitch" on the internet is the last straw.

After crying, I still had scabby elbows and a foggy perception of reality, but after a little pressure was released, I did feel a bit better. My view of reality stopped being quite so distorted.

I know I have a loving family and true friends who care. I know that periods of being down will pass. I know the number of reviews my book has doesn't determine my worth, nor was anyone slighting me by not reviewing it. They're just doing their thing in life, same as me. Who really has time for *another* book in their queue?

Still, though, I would like to learn how to not cry just so I can save my tears for when I'm alone so that I don't have to make everyone else uncomfortable.

At the very least, hopefully they don't feel like I'm using tears to manipulate them. [2]

---

[2] Am I using this chapter to manipulate my friends and family into reviewing my books? No, because they probably aren't reading this book either. Zing!

THREE

Too Sensitive

Has someone ever criticized you by saying you were *too sensitive*? Being sensitive sucks sometimes and even creates situations where people feel like they're walking on eggshells around you. It's hard to be someone who is easily hurt. But you know what? The world needs sensitive people! Can you imagine a world with no sensitive people? Being sensitive might be the quality that also makes you thoughtful, kind and artistic. Being sensitive is not all bad! So, next time someone derisively calls you "too sensitive," tell them you're not "too sensitive" for them to bite you sideways.

SILLY DEPRESSED

FOUR

Childhood Depression

"I don't feel good."

It was a pretty decent summation and it was true. I was 8 years old and I didn't feel good. I felt sad, but since I didn't have anything specific to feel sad about- I thought I was sick.

"I don't feel good," I said to my teacher for the umpteenth time.

She raised her voice.

"What. Do you want. Me to do about it?!"

She was fed up. She didn't see a child with chronic problems in need of coping skills and professional help. She saw a whiner. I was annoying her.

SILLY DEPRESSED

After she said that, I walked away in silence, hot with shame.

It was clear to me then. *I feel bad and no one can do anything about it, so that's that.*

The school had no psychologist or even a nurse. That's life, kid! It's gray, joyless and the ugly butterflies in your stomach aren't going anywhere.

That same teacher once gave me a panic attack. She passed out a pop quiz. We had never had a pop quiz before. That was something that only happened on *Saved by the Bell*! My insides turned to jelly. I looked at the paper she passed out and my heart started thumping. My face burned. I didn't recognize any of the material on the quiz. After a minute of total emotional abandonment, she interrupted.

"Ha ha! April fools!" she said.

"Ohhhh! Ha! I was gonna say...! I was like, what's this?!" some of the other kids said. They were taking it in stride like it wasn't the end of the world while I, and probably a few others, felt our souls leaving our bodies.

Who made you feel trapped when you were a kid? Who made you feel like there was no possibility of ever feeling any better? Draw a picture of them high-fiving my teacher. If you are using a tablet, gently flick my teacher on the face.[3]

---

[3] Now that I've spoken my truth, I forgive her. She was young, didn't have resources, may have been tired that day, might be more compassionate now, blah blah blah.

That same year I had a panic attack that involved puffy paint. I attended a girls club called Busy Bees in a church gymnasium. It echoed with the excitement of a hundred girls, which was much too loud for me. We were decorating sweatshirts with puffy paint and sparkly plastic gems. I was trying to glue a gem when a grown-up saw me struggling. I wasn't cool enough to know how puffy paint attire was supposed to look. She squeezed a huge amount of paint into a puddle on the sweatshirt and smushed the gem into it. The paint oozed around the sides of the gem. It was supposed to look like that, but it was unexpected and somehow that made me feel like I was in a dream. I didn't want or expect gooey neon paint drowning my beautiful multifaceted gem! Of course, I swallowed my feelings. When my mom picked me up, I told her I felt like I wasn't really there. Like I was in a dream. She acknowledged my feelings and didn't make me go back again.

Sidenote: At this same girls club, there was a rumor going around about a girl who ATE HER BOOK. We had workbooks with bible verses and assignments you could earn badges for. Apparently this girl ate the whole thing- piece by piece. It totally blew my unstable little mind! I wondered if that girl was getting the professional help that I needed. Eating an entire book makes a bigger statement than saying "I don't feel good." Damn it, I should have eaten a book.

My parents loved me, but didn't really know I was suffering. I was often quiet and, thanks to my dismissive teacher, I had no idea any kind of help was available. I thought life just felt bad.

As I entered middle school, I lashed out. I got obnoxious and disrespectful. I told my friend Emily that I never had good days. I felt bad every day and some days were just slightly better than others. Emily would sometimes get to leave school early to see a counselor because her parents were divorced. At least *someone* got help.

Another sidenote: Emily and I wrote *Friends* fanfiction. After the end of season one, when we were dying to find out what was going to happen with Ross and Rachel, we continued the story on our own and read it aloud to one another. I wish to God that I still had that bit of writing.

In high school, I found some people to kind of fit in with, but always had the nagging feeling of being an outsider who couldn't connect with very many people. To top it off, I thought it was a good idea to style myself as a punk with unflattering clothes and haircuts. I was also hanging around some very pretty friends who garnered the attention of all the boys I wished would pay attention to me. Why was not my spiky hair stealing their hearts? And what of my studded belts? Ripped up jeans? Converse All Stars? Ironic thrift store shirts? It was just the awkward topping on my dish of existential-dread-flavored froyo.

Speaking of which, I became lactose intolerant around that time. Didn't love it.

I didn't get help until I was 17 [4] and was crying so much that I was debilitated.

---

[4] Pictured: Me, a teenager. This is the best picture I have of my Karen hair.

SILLY DEPRESSED

I remember sitting at the top of the stairs one morning crying, unable to stop. I couldn't go to school. That's when I was finally diagnosed with major depression and medicated with a drug that, for me personally, was the absolute devil- Venlafaxine.[5]

---

[5] Can I get sued for saying this? Like, look Venlafaxine people, I've never profited off my writing. I've spent more on writing than I've made. Probably no one is even reading this. Please don't sue, thanks, and also- bite me sideways.

FIVE

Venlafaxine

Venlafaxine worked great for me. It subdued my clinical depression so I could be freed up to be depressed about real stuff and never improve myself. Here's the thing though, if I missed a dose, and I mean miss it by even a few hours, I got something called "brain zaps."

For me, brain zaps didn't literally feel like an electric shock in my brain. It felt like my perception of reality was a skipping vinyl record. It was disorienting and panic-inducing.

24 hours after a missed dose, I could count on having a total breakdown from the withdrawal. I once left home for the weekend and forgot to take

the medication with me and I remember the drive back home was spent sobbing in the back seat of a Corolla. My sister and best friend must have been bewildered. It's not great to have someone openly weeping in a small space and to have no way of helping them. I could call them and ask if they remember this experience, but I hope they don't and I don't actually want to know if they do. Reliving it in one paragraph is enough for me.

With withdrawal symptoms being so severe, I must have taken it for one period of time and then never again, right? No! I ended up taking Venlafaxine three different times in my life because when it works, it's awesome!

The last period of withdrawal I had was just before getting TMS for the first time (more on that later) and it was so severe that this time, for real, I won't take it ever again. In part it was doubly bad, because I was also going through withdrawal from some Adderall that I took for a short time. I was in bed for weeks and kept a diary of my symptoms.

Thursday, 5/17, Day 1: brain zaps.

Friday, 5/18, Day 2: sobbing, brain zaps.

Saturday, 5/19, Day 3: no Adderall, sobbing, brain zaps, hot flashes, chills, insomnia, existential agony, night sweats, anxiety, disorientation, feeling hopeless and like my life will never amount to anything and I'm only a burden on others, fatigue.

KRISTIN HOOKER

Fatigue at the end makes me laugh.

Sunday, 5/20, Day 4: took 10mg Adderall at noon because I worried I was experiencing double withdrawal, crying, hopelessness, nausea, fatigue, brain zaps, and disorientation. Felt a little better after taking Adderall. Took Adderall again at 5 PM and drank about an ounce of vodka. Still dizzy, disoriented, fatalistic. Insomnia, irritability.

Don't ask me why I threw an ounce of vodka into the mix. No idea. Maybe I thought I was going through alcohol withdrawal too?

Monday, 5/21, Day 5: 10mg Adderall at 9 AM, crying before it's even 10 AM. Hopelessness, brain zaps, disorientation, lack of focus, feeling guilty about how much of a burden I am. Another 10mg Adderall at 3 PM, weeping and despair, inability to drive, irritability.

Tuesday, 5/22, Day 6: crying, brain zaps, disorientation, lack of focus, irritability, loss of appetite.
Wednesday, 5/23, Day 7: light crying, brain zaps.

Thursday, 5/24, Day 8: lack of motivation, light crying, brain zaps, fatigue, irritability, disorientation.

Friday, 5/25, Day 9: irritability, cramps, nightmares, brain zaps, crying.

-No Adderall from here on; 300mg

SILLY DEPRESSED

Wellbutrin, Ativan as needed.

Saturday, 5/26, Day 10: brain zaps, irritability, cannot handle any stress at all, (overall very irritable and emotional, anxious, but brain zaps and disorientation improved), difficulty falling asleep without Ativan.

Sunday, 5/27, Day 11: woke with energy for a few hours then felt down, wanted to be alone, brain zaps every few hours, a little irritable, but not raging, fearful about the world, crying.

Monday, 5/28, Day 12: first day starting supplements, took a 30 min. walk, fatigued, depressed, want to stay in bed, made it through holiday cookout, but felt awful after eating sugar. Only a few brain zaps.

Tuesday, 5/29, Day 13: energy briefly in morning, then fatigued, dizzy, heavy feeling, brain zaps, crying, able to pick up son alone and make some phone calls.

Wednesday, 5/30, Day 14: has to take Ativan to sleep at night, dizzy, brain zaps, tearful, chills.

Notice the switch to third person? It was like I was dissociating and turning myself into a little scientist who takes notes instead of being the person who was actually feeling all this stuff.

Thursday, 5/31, Day 15: brain zaps, dizziness, depressed, anxious or morbid thoughts, lack of concentration or clear thinking, feeling of unreality, inability to handle stress, imagining distressing situations.

-Increased Wellbutrin to 450mg

Friday, 6/1, Day 16: regretted the splash of coffee I had. I think it triggered zaps and an energy crash, anxious, depressed, unfocused, hard time driving and talking at the same time, cannot handle stress.

Saturday, 6/2, Day 17: drank water at breakfast, no caffeine and I haven't had brain zaps yet, very hard to concentrate, spacey, blue, some zaps, so sleepy, Ativan.

Sunday, 6/3, Day 18: feeling relaxed this morning, but low energy. Not super anxious, just foggy. Conversation is a struggle. Today wasn't horrible. Low level brain zaps. Had a glass of chardonnay on a date.

Do you think the date was fun? I'm willing to bet it wasn't great.

Monday, 6/4, Day 19: feel low key. Took a long walk. Daydreaming a lot. Hard to concentrate or stay on task. Mildly sad.

Tuesday, 6/5, Day 20: woke groggy. Spent the morning alone, driving, listening to music, have the gigs. Mentally sloppy, but not sad. Crazy mood swing after lunch. Crazy mood swing after dinner.

SILLY DEPRESSED

Daydreaming constantly. Brain zaps.

Wednesday, 6/6, Day 21: OK morning. Tired after going out. I put makeup on today. Daydreaming. Brain zaps. Giggling to crying this afternoon. Crash after dinner.

Thursday, 6/7, Day 22: just sad all day.

Friday, 6/8, Day 23: spent the morning feeling NOTHING. Afternoon tearful and sad. All I could do was try to go to sleep. Couldn't fall asleep. Feel vast emptiness. When will this end? Brain zaps.

Saturday, 6/9, Day 24: woke OK, fell into depression mid-morning and stayed there. Can't bear the thought of continuing to feel this way indefinitely. It's just not possible. I feel like I'm not suicidal now, but eventually I will be. The withdrawal symptoms like irritability and brain zaps are nearly gone, but I'm left with depression, lack of concentration, daydreaming, low energy.

Thankfully I never made it to suicidal.

Sunday, 6/10, Day 25: sad, tears, low energy, headache.

Monday, 6/11, Day 26: brain zaps, unfocused, not terrible day, but I crashed after dinner. Totally out of it.

Tuesday, 6/12, Day 27: mild brain zaps, unfocused, daydreamy, not terrible.

Wednesday, 6/13, Day 28: mild zaps, unfocused, can't handle stress, feel like the world is ending, spacey, sad, obsessive thoughts about choking on things or saying embarrassing things.

Thursday, 6/14, Day 29: dread, panicky feeling. Starting antipsychotic.

Friday, 6/15, Day 30: sad all morning, hopeless, energy picked up in afternoon, brain zaps.

Saturday, 6/16, Day 31: SO HAZY. Hopeless feeling.

Since I stopped taking notes, I imagine it must have gotten a little less intense.

About two months later, I would start TMS and that would change my life. Again, more on that later.

SILLY DEPRESSED

SIX

Unwanted Thoughts

My first unwanted thought came when I was a teenager. I stood at the kitchen counter under some cabinets and imagined bashing my head into the corner. I didn't want to do it. I didn't want to think about it. But I couldn't stop thinking about it! Every time I stood at the counter, that corner mocked me.

Later in life, I went through a period where the unwanted thoughts were about public humiliation. My mind, being a real a-hole, would be like *"Hey! What if you just kind of said some derogatory words to some people?"*

"No! Why? I would never! That's like, one of

the worst things I can imagine!"

"*I know. Mwahahaha!*"

"Stop it!"

"*Oh, I know! Picture this: You meet a celebrity you admire and ask them to give you money.*"

"That's the tackiest shit I can think of!"

"*Yup!*"

For a period of about a month when I was going through Venlafaxine withdrawal, these thoughts were constant. They were agonizing.

My unwanted thoughts are a real creep.

SILLY DEPRESSED

In addition to those public humiliation thoughts, I had a nagging feeling that I was in someone else's house, so whenever I was looking for anything, I felt like the *real* homeowner was about to arrive home and catch me rifling through all their stuff. My brain produced a harrowing short film where they catch me red-handed in their drawers looking for a pen and they accuse me of stealing and the police are on their way right now!

WEEE-OOOH WEEE-OOOH

"YOU'RE GOING TO PRISON. What was that? You thought you were in *your house*? In that case, you're going to a FREEZING COLD VICTORIAN ERA ASYLUM where only the craziest ones say they're not crazy!"

In times of transition, the unwanted thoughts and depression become worse. In 2010, I was newly wed and left my day job to become a writer. Even though these changes were good, I was anxious a lot and my unwanted thoughts rose to a new level:

Obsession.

I was obsessed with the idea that I was going to accidentally drop a knife on a baby.

I had no baby. There were no babies around. I wasn't a habitual knife dropper. I worried and worried though! I felt guilty and ashamed that I had dropped a knife on a baby, even though it had never happened. The images kept running through my mind. I would be standing at the counter cutting a vegetable. A baby would crawl onto my feet. I would fumble the knife and it would clatter on the counter and topple over the edge. Boom. Cut baby! A baby has been cut! Did you hurt the baby?! Feel shame forever!

When I had unwanted thoughts, I would compulsively close my eyes really tight and whisper "fuck." I didn't particularly want to do this. It didn't make me feel better. I just kind of did it.

That year wasn't the only year I had unwanted, obsessive thoughts. In 2018 when I was alone in the car driving to TMS worried I would somehow commit vehicular manslaughter, I would grip the steering wheel and shout "FUCK!"

It still didn't really make me feel better. I just did it because I felt I had to.

In film and television, OCD is always centered on someone with rituals and it's presented as quirky. *Uh-oh, looks like we've got a germophobe! Look at how superstitious the guy who won't step on cracks is.*

In reality it's not so cinematic. It's not quirky and it's never fun.

When the thoughts come, I mentally run and when I run I experience the cringe. The cringe is hard, fast and sharp like lightning. I feel it in my gut and scrunch up my face. When I have the courage to sit with the thought, it feels different. It's slow, round and gray. It's like a cloud that forms and dissipates like breath. I ask the thought what it's trying to tell me and usually it has a lesson like "Be vigilant when you drive" or "Choose your words with care," so I try with all my might to flip the thought into a good thing.

Why don't we have obsessive thoughts about

good things? Obsessing over anything is unpleasant even if it *is* good, but what if you could look into the mirror and think obsessively about how beautiful your skin is instead of having the impulse to pick it to scabs? Can we program those in? Let's try! Repeat these thoughts and then next time your brain spins out of control, maybe you'll think about these nice things instead.

Dear God, I'm beautiful.

The only objects inside my body cavities are the ones that are supposed to be there.

I always seem to say the right thing.

I've totally never sharted and never will and so I shall eat as many cheese-stuffed dates as I want.

I'm so good at driving- I once used an unfinished overpass as a ramp and landed at my house.

I'm real and made of organic matter, and that matter? Utter perfection.

My genitals never get snagged on anything, they really know how to stay put.

Write down the opposites of your unwanted thoughts.

I'll start.

I'm in my house and everything in this house is mine. I'm right where I'm supposed to be.

SILLY DEPRESSED

SEVEN

The Giggles

There was once a turning point where I was starting to see the light at the end of the tunnel and then I struggled with the giggles. I had just gotten LASIK and I asked the woman who answered the phone at the clinic if it was OK to rub my eyes yet and she said I should never rub my eyes.

"Like, ever again?" I asked.

"You should never rub your eyes, ever," she said in a very serious, urgent tone.

This seemed strange to me and she wasn't a doctor, so the next time I went in for a check-up to see how my eyes were healing, I asked the doctor.

"The woman on the phone told me I could never rub my eyes again, ever."

I started giggling. It seemed like such a dramatic thing to say.

The doctor giggled a little. He saw the humor in it. Then he told me something about rubbing my eyes, but I can't remember what, because I was giggling and focusing very hard on trying to not giggle.

I would succeed momentarily, but then a minute later, the doctor would have one of those eyeball exam things up against my face and his face would be about two inches from mine and then I'd start giggling again.

After that, I went out to lunch with my husband and mother-in-law. The giggles came back and of course, I had to explain what I thought was so funny. These things are never funny to anyone but me.

Then I went home and thought my giggle fit deserved to be immortalized in a video, so I turned on my camera and started telling the giggle story. Every time I tried to explain it, I'd laugh harder until I started crying.

The fact that I was able to laugh seemed like a good sign. And it was.

The crying wasn't great, but I was on my way to getting better. Small victories add up.

SILLY DEPRESSED

EIGHT

A Reason To Be Depressed Comes Along

An entry from my diary dated March 29, 2020
*

I've had chronic depression, on and off my whole life. When the depression comes along, there's no situation in my life causing it. When I feel that sinking feeling start to develop in my chest, I know what to do- I call the doctor. We decide on a treatment, whether it's drugs or TMS. We do the treatment. If it doesn't work, we try something else. I always get better, eventually.

If I were depressed because of something happening in the real world that I had any degree of control over, I could come up with a course of action. I would call a therapist and talk it out. I would clean up my habits and make sure I'm giving myself a hearty dose of positive self-talk.

I am, however, depressed because of something happening in the real world that I have no control over. No medication will help. No action on my part will truly make a dent in this situation. I am depressed because I can't go anywhere or see anyone. Plans that I was looking forward to were canceled and won't be rescheduled. My son had his last day of preschool EVER and when it happened, I didn't even know it was his last day. I don't know if he'll get to start kindergarten in September. I don't know when I'll be able to see my family members again.

Admittedly, I have it pretty easy. We have food. We are not in danger of "losing everything." Nevertheless, I'm a little depressed and having perspective doesn't seem to help.

I love reaching out to people with depression and encouraging them to get help. I love reassuring them that they will find a treatment that works.

What can I say to this kind of depression? There's no cure. What if we do everything we can- exercise, eat healthy, stay in touch with people on the phone, make art- and we still don't feel better? At that point, we have to accept that we are depressed and just allow ourselves to feel it. We don't like uncomfortable feelings. When we have them, we run away or try to fix them or smother them with pleasure.

This time, discomfort has us cornered. For

some it's worse than others, but we're all at least a little uncomfortable and we have to sit with those feelings. There's nothing wrong with being depressed when there's a reason to be depressed. We just have to let it run its course.

*

That diary entry was written when COVID-19 was just starting. Having a tangible reason to be depressed was somewhat new to me. I had to mourn losses: The loss of opportunities for my son to have a fun childhood (though to be honest, he liked being home all the time). The loss of his entire kindergarten year. The loss of those tickets to see *The Dollop*. The loss of time with family and friends. The loss of trips to the movies and date nights. The loss of my favorite restaurants closing forever.

Of course, those are relatively small disappointments.

Others had to mourn the loss of friends and family members. The loss of jobs. The loss of a home. The loss of security. Worsening social conditions. Troubles much more serious than my own.

The world became brittle and agitated.

We, the medicated, couldn't run from these feelings of sadness or fear.

All we could do was try to cope.

SILLY DEPRESSED

NINE

Am I Depressed Or Am I Just a Morbid Weirdo?

How many morbid thoughts are too many? Are there actually people who *don't* think about death every damn day?

Even when I'm happy, I still think about death several times a day. I have a feeling if I told a psychiatrist this, they might be alarmed. I think about what it feels like to die. I think about how I would feel if people I love died. Even though I've never truly had the desire to end my life, I still think about it plenty, just wondering.

Here's a theory- when you grow up being told that "your friends who aren't Christians would go to hell if they died today," you tend to get anxious about death. I mean, dear God. If my beloved pal steps into the street at the wrong moment, she's going to be tortured forever?!

SILLY DEPRESSED

Or is that just a Christian fan theory put out there by Dante? Some fan theories take on a life of their own.

Evangelicals talk about mortality A LOT and maybe they just got my brain into the habit.

More than anything, I'm just confused about death. I listen to a lot of ghost stories and I'm unsure what the rules are. Some people on their deathbeds see other-worldly entities or already deceased loved ones shortly before they die, as if that being has been sent to usher them away.

Some people are visited by loved ones shortly after that loved one dies. They can come in bodily form, dreams, smells, sounds, and feelings.

Some ghosts get to travel wherever they want; others are stuck someplace.

Some of them are cruel; others miraculously save people's lives.

Some of them replay scenes from their life like a looped video.

Some people have near death experiences and describe entering heaven and being greeted by loved ones who tell them to go back to earth.

I once used a ouija board with my friend EB and the spirit told us it was the spirit of an aborted baby and I believed it. We asked that ghost to scare a guy from school that we didn't like. It told us that it was dragging underwear around his house to scare him. That will do, baby ghost, thanks. EB told me much later on that she was moving the planchet. I felt betrayed. Baby ghosts, though? What *are* baby ghosts doing?

Where are the cavemen ghosts? Do ghosts expire? I heard about the ghost of Anne Boleyn doing spooky shit and she was alive hundreds of years ago, yet they never tell stories about ghosts from ancient times.

Mormons say they get their own planet with their family. I asked my friend what happens if he doesn't marry before he dies and he said there's a loophole- a planet for single people.

If Dante and whoever wrote the *Left Behind* series can have Christian fan theories, why can't I? Here's what I think is a possibility:

We spend eternity cleaning up the mess we made.

I mean this in the best possible way.

We all go to Heaven, then God sends us back down to a new earth with no more pain or sorrow and we cheerfully dig up every last bit of plastic we put in the ground. We rewild the world. We live in harmony with the animals. We climb mountains, build our own log cabins and travel the world with bodies that never get tired.

It's encouraging to me to believe that if I don't get to witness the aurora borealis in this lifetime, I'll get to later. The Mediterranean will still be waiting for me. I can still learn an instrument. I don't have to feel a sense of panic about what I don't achieve in this life. Maybe my constant thoughts about death are actually a positive thing.

Or maybe I'm just a morbid weirdo.

SILLY DEPRESSED

TEN

Bed

The best place in the world! I'm writing this book in my bed and I'm not even depressed right now. And if bed is like a big warm roll when I'm happy, it's like a big warm roll with melty butter when I'm depressed.

Everything happens on that bed. My son climbs onto it in the morning. The day he was born, my water broke on it. I spend the morning getting my son ready for school, but when I'm relieved of that duty, I head straight back to my bed to figure out what I'm doing next and fill out my day planner. It's home base!

At night I hang out with my husband on it,

talking and watching TV. He brings video games and instruments to bed so we can do separate things together.

I fold laundry on it.

I've cried on it while falling asleep because I've made up some awful, sad scenario in my head that feels too real.

I once woke up and found a flattened spider on it that I apparently laid on all night.

My dog gets on the bed, because it's her favorite place too.

It is comfort. It's where I receive unconscious relief from my angst.

The flip side is that it is also where I receive the creeping guilty feeling that it is a forbidden place in the middle of the day.

I'm supposed to be productive all day. Taking a break is shameful. Naps are for losers! But just look at that warm, velvety blanket.

Sometimes my dog starts barking at me to play. It's really naughty, but the only way I can get her to stop is to pretend to fall asleep, also known as *actually* falling asleep.

Whoops I took a three hour nap!

I'm going out tonight and will probably stay out one hour past my bedtime which means I need a preparatory rest.

Whoops I took a three hour nap!

I feel like I might be coming down with a cold or something. I know!- I'll take a "whoopsItookathreehournap."

I put on a movie for my son, I might as well snuggle up and...whoops I took a two hour nap plus a one hour period of moaning in response to my son repeatedly shaking me and asking me to play Lego. Whoops!

I ate a big bowl of pasta at lunch.

Naps are normal in Spain.

I'll set an alarm for twenty minutes.

I'll be so productive when I wake up.

Whoops!

I can't judge if you have time or need for a nap, only you can. If you decide that you have time and need for a nap, try telling yourself this:

I can acknowledge that my mental and emotional anguish takes a physical toll on my body. I'll try to forge ahead, but when I can't, I'll be kind to myself if I need to rest instead. Taking a nap doesn't mean I'm lazy, giving up, or giving in.

Go ahead. Appreciate that bed. It really is the best place.

SILLY DEPRESSED

ELEVEN

IDGAF

I remember back in college leaving a male friend's house late at night to walk home and I evaluated my decision to walk down a dark alley.

It's like, maybe I'll make it home OK, or maybe I'll get murdered. Whatever.

And, while I was clearly depressed, I didn't feel particularly depressed at that moment. I felt like a woman with nothing to lose.

Free.

(And somehow those absolute sweethearts of male friends didn't offer to walk me home.)

Another day, I was walking on my college campus with a rolled up poster and wondered what would happen if I bopped a stranger on the head with it.

So I did it.

"Heeeeeeeey!" he complained.

To that man, I am sorry. I wasn't considering your feelings. How rude!

Not giving a fuck makes you feel free to do uncomfortable things.

I repeatedly saw the first *Harry Potter* movie in the theater, alone, and sometimes the place was even empty. I ran into an acquaintance in the parking lot of the theater. She pitied me for being alone, but I wasn't sure why. I was going to watch *Harry Potter* and could leave before the movie was even over, if I felt like it. Nothing matters!

I went into a lecture hall and sat directly next to someone even though there were literally hundreds of empty seats available, just to be weird. The woman I sat next to moved away from me and fanned her face with a paper as though she were too hot to sit next to someone.

How insufferable was I?

I went on weird dates with weird men from *OK Cupid*, which isn't terribly safe, but what the hell, why not? I went out with a guy a few times who ended up taking me on a walk in an unfamiliar neighborhood and then refused to tell me how to get back to my car. This was back when I didn't have an iPhone to map my way. OK, maybe that one's not funny.

At times of IDGAF depression, I have willfully put myself in odd situations just to see what may happen and, while it's sometimes obnoxious, other times it just gives me something to write about.

Have you ever done something weird because you were depressed and just didn't care about social mores? Please tell me.

SILLY DEPRESSED

TWELVE

Advice

"Maybe you need vitamins."

"Exercise is supposed to help."

"Drink more water."

"You have to carry on."

"You don't look depressed. I saw you smile yesterday."

"Some people have actual problems."

"This too shall pass."

In those moments, I feel like I'm naked and cold and someone is handing me a single sock, but it's all they have. They're not a professional. They don't have a blanket.

They might be someone who loves you who

can't stand to see you suffering and they just want to help somehow.

Or they might be an absolute stranger who doesn't know shit about crap.

Here's a comment someone left for me on one of my *YouTube* videos about my experience with depression.

LOL My parents came here with $50 in their pocket as immigrants. My mom raised 3 children while going to medical school, took care of my father, laundry, cooking - the whole nine. Full-time doctor the last 25 years, retiring in a few. It's amazing how people see no correlation between stay-at-home "mom and wife" and depression. Serious 1st world problems.

Cool. Your mom sounds awesome.

I guess since I'm experiencing first world problems, I don't deserve to get my depression treated even though treatment is available, is that how it works? Also, it sounds like you think stay-at-home moms aren't performing labor. Seeing as how your mom is a doctor who also does domestic labor, you should ask for her opinion about these things. I'd love to hear what she has to say.

What is the worst comment or advice you've received about your depression?

SILLY DEPRESSED

KRISTIN HOOKER

THIRTEEN

Nothing Is Fun

This is a photo of me visiting a fun farm. See my face in the background?

SILLY DEPRESSED

The farm has a trampoline, a little train, a petting zoo, and you can watch a baby cow be born in a theater setting. I had my son in tow along with other various relatives.

In this picture, we had gotten on a bus that was taking us to a pig farm. Unbeknownst to me, I was captured in the background of a selfie my brother and sister were taking. My normally round face is angular. As I stare into the center distance, I am probably fantasizing about like, *What if I was really good looking and could also afford an intricately tiled in-ground hot tub and also be happy and popular?*

None of the supposedly *fun* activities were any fun at all and to top it off, the farm was later exposed for abusing animals.

I stopped drinking alcohol because that wasn't fun. Watching TV wasn't fun. Eating wasn't

fun. I never operated a Jetski, but I'm willing to bet that wouldn't have been fun either.

I kept seeing friends for game night.

I kept mingling at children's birthday parties.

I kept watching movies and going to restaurants and roller skating.

I might as well have been sitting and staring at a wall because that would have been equally as fun.

Here's the kicker- you might keep doing all these non-fun things because if you don't, you're afraid people will forget you even exist or they might think you're a downer. You think, *One of these days I'm going to feel better and I'd like to still have friends when that happens. Also, my young child deserves to have fun. So here, have some fun.*

I'll show up. Let's do the fun.

The funnest thing I've ever done while depressed was go to a *Medieval Times Dinner and Tournament*. I waved a little green flag. I clapped for my friend's birthday announcement. I forced a smile on the waiter who came to me asking "Pepsi, M'lady?"

It all felt so ludicrous.

What's the "funnest" thing you've done while depressed?

SILLY DEPRESSED

KRISTIN HOOKER

FOURTEEN

You Are An Alien Pretending To Be Human

You've been invited to a thing. You're psyching yourself up to act normal. On your planet, casual conversation is not customary. Your customs include burrowing under blankets, eating processed food so you don't have to cook, sniffing laundry because you can't remember if it's clean, and watching movies with your partner so you don't have to talk and can just sit there and think about the futility of life.

First you must choose an outfit. You don't know if socks are supposed to show around your ankle parts. Are the humans doing bare ankles? Or

SILLY DEPRESSED

socked ankles? You saw a teen human the other day with socks and sandals. Yeah. Socks and sandals must be "in."

You arrive on time in your socks and sandals assuming that the sooner you arrive, the sooner you can leave and minimize the risk of being exposed as an alien. You've made a huge mistake. Your plan was to stand on the edge of other people's conversations, but that won't be possible for quite some time since there's hardly anyone here yet.

You set a gift on a table, then freeze. How do they stand when they have nothing specific to do? You cram your hands into your pockets in hopes that you look nonchalant.

Now raise your facial features! Chin up, eyebrows up, corners of mouth up!

An acquaintance is walking towards you. They're going to ask what you've been up to! What do you say?! Fill this template with relevant information.

I've been _____! Busy, busy, busy. So many projects around my house. I've started watching videos about remodeling my _____. I've been getting really into _____. Oh, and I'm planning a trip to _____. How are you?
(Pause and listen)

Let me tell you, before I have a social event, appointment or any situation where I might see someone I know and have to talk to them, I feel like I'm in this waiting room. Like all I can think about is the coming event. Like I can't accomplish anything while I wait. I just ruminate, trying to ready myself. And what am I so anxious about?

That I won't have anything to say and that people will think I'm boring or weird.

Here's the thing though- ruminating ahead of time doesn't change any of that. Ruminating doesn't give me more things to talk about or change my personality or life situation. So why not carry on? I can live my life and then when the event comes, I'll say what I have to say. I'll focus on the other person, be kind to them, and if they think I'm weird, who cares?

If a social occasion is going to suck so much energy away, I can't afford to let it suck away energy in the day leading up to it too.

Afterall, I'm an alien with things to do.

SILLY DEPRESSED

KRISTIN HOOKER

FIFTEEN

A Metaphor With Swimming

You know how to swim like a pro. You glide around the deep end, say hi to the kids at the shallow end, and you're really good at that game where you try to talk underwater. It's a great place to say swear words like *shitbag*.

    Then one day someone over in the deep end says "Hey! Come over here!"

    You start cruising in that direction. Or at least you try. Something is wrong. Were you always this slow? Are you just tired? Come to think of it, you've been getting tired a lot lately.

    Wow, it's hard to swim right now.

    What's weighing you down?

SILLY DEPRESSED

You look through the distortion of the water and you see weights around your ankles. The weights are part of you. They grew slowly like tumors and now are pulling you down like sandbags. Fleshy disgusting sandbags.

Well shit.

You know how to swim, you're trying to swim, but it's not going so great.

So what are you going to do about it? You go to a doctor and she lists 25 different treatments you can try to get rid of them. All of the treatments work for some people, none of the treatments work for everyone, and several will give you diarrhea.

Good luck!

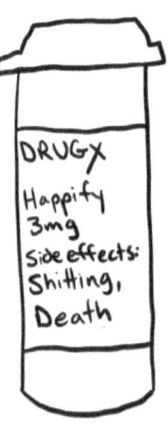

SIXTEEN

All The Treatments!

A list of treatments I've tried:
Please keep in mind that just because a treatment didn't work for me, that doesn't mean it won't work for someone else. These are just my personal experiences.

Abilify - Jury is still out on this one. It's an antipsychotic used to boost the effects of your regular antidepressants. I currently take it and it might be making me more focused. Who the hell knows anymore?

Adderall - To me, it was just slightly

mellower Ritalin. *See Ritalin.*

Cannabis - I used a CBD tincture with some THC to soothe panic attacks. It succeeded in removing the weight I felt in my chest, but my thoughts were still plagued by climate change-induced famine. Of course, it's not really *about* climate change famine. I was panicking for no particular reason and then my brain just picked something. After climate change terrors wore off, I became terrified I would leave my son someplace and just lose him. Cannabis could not make these thoughts go away.

Fluoxetine - Everyone's favorite! Americans take so much of it that our bodily waste has transferred the drug to our water supply. Now the fish are happy too![6] I don't recall how many years I took it, but after it pooped out, I got back with my toxic ex-boyfriend Venlafaxine.

Lexapro - Lexapro gives me my sparkle. It keeps my anxiety in check, makes me more focused, and since it has somewhat severe withdrawal effects, I'm pretty much going to stay on it forever!

Olanzapine - Never have I known such clarity. Never have I known such hunger. Olanzapine is an antipsychotic that my doctor offered me after I told him I had a daydreaming problem. I had such trouble with focus and brain fog, my mind retreated to imagination, but it was imagination without control. My sad made-up thoughts would make me cry. Olanzapine almost instantly swept away the cobwebs of my dark

---

[6] I'm aware Fluoxetine is not good for the fish.

thoughts and I was finally able to be present.

Present and hungry as hell.

The hunger felt like I had just run for miles and it never went away. I rapidly gained about five pounds.

The final straw was a night where in a dark kitchen I hunched over a bucket of alphabet cookies shoveling them into my mouth. It was the first time in my life I felt shame around food.

I stopped taking it.

Ritalin - I recall the first day that I took Ritalin. I was taking my son to a birthday party- an occasion that is sometimes awkward. While the children have their party, there is a second party happening and the second party is made up of parents who lost a coin toss with their partner that morning.

On this day, though? I popped a Ritalin and I COULD NOT WAIT to go to this shindig. I wanted to talk to EVERYONE: The grandparents of the birthday girl. The teacher who only rides a bike. The lady who makes artisanal vegan cheese.

With Ritalin, I felt amazing.

For about a week.

After that, I started crashing after it wore off and I needed Ritalin just to feel not terrible. The romance was gone. I'm sure it's not like that for everyone, but it was bad for me and, thankfully, I had enough sense to quit.

Venlafaxine - You know about this one already. Bastard.

Wellbutrin - Wellbutrin does exactly what you'd expect. It makes me feel well. Not good. Not great. Well. Fine, thanks. My Wellbutrin wellness is buttressed by my Abilify abilities and my Lexapro sparkle.

The downside? The first week I took it, I broke out in hives every day.

Counseling - By far, this one takes the most emotional effort. I'm tired just thinking about writing about it. If I went today, I'd probably cry the whole drive home and feel guilty for burdening another human with an hour (honestly, 50 minutes) of crying and whining about myself.

Let's leave it at that.

Faith Healing - No, I'm not kidding. Other than saying my own prayers, I once drove through a snowstorm to see a couple who were involved in faith healing ministry. The man said that he had once had an inoperable brain tumor. They went to a faith healing group and the tumor disappeared. They considered it a miracle.

When they asked about my family history and any possible occult activity, they were concerned that I once found Freemason rings in my grandmother's treasure-filled basement. The concern was that maybe a hereditary demon was causing the panic attacks.

I reserved judgment because I was willing to try anything to feel better and would hang on to any shred of hope that I could.

The only thing that happened that I can't exactly explain is that while they were praying for me, I started having back spasms. I tried not to, but my resistance was futile.

And you know what? I still had panic attacks.

Probably like, the next day and every day after that for a long time.

Hypnotherapy - Hypnotherapy was to help get more control over my thoughts and, I gotta say, I loved it. A woman in jersey earth-tones would sit cross-legged on a desk chair while I leaned back in a zero gravity lounger covered in a blanket. She guided me through vivid thoughts, ones in which I walked down flights of stairs into rooms with things like projectors with my memories imprinted on film that I could set on fire if I wanted to. I bundled my thoughts into my hands and placed them in magical trunks that caused them to disappear. I retreated to lakes and forests to find peace. I learned visualizations that I still use to this day.

Neurofeedback - I spent about a thousand dollars renting a neurofeedback set-up from my counselor. I don't know how it works, but I can tell you what it looks like. I would set up a laptop that played videos that looked like *Windows 95* screensavers. Simultaneously, I had headphones on with peaceful music, but beneath the music there were barely perceptible clicks. Somehow those clicks were supposed to do something to reorganize my messy, foggy, negative mind.

I used it every day for a month for about a half hour each time.

The amount of good it did was, in my opinion, worth about seventy-five bucks, not a thousand.

Sensory Deprivation - I went to a float tank exactly one time. For the uninitiated, a float tank is a dark, giant enclosed bathtub with 10 inches of water saturated with Epsom salt. You effortlessly float in water that is, and this is key- the same temperature as your skin, about 93 degrees Fahrenheit. That way, you feel nothing.

Nothing!

Just you and your thoughts.

I paid for 90 minutes, but probably only stayed for 45. I wanted to enjoy it, but I just really wanted it to be warmer. I know, that would defeat the purpose!

I should have gone to the spa instead.

Spa - During one of my lowest times, I booked a spa. I didn't feel like it, but I peeled my body off my bed and ventured to the spa above the Burnside Skatepark. It was the kind of spa where you sit in warm water, then hot water, then ludicrously cold water, then a steam room, then a dry sauna, and then you do it all over again. It smells amazing and there are barrels of herby water to drink. I eased into hot water, gazed out at the cloudy sky and thought *I was sad at home, now I'm sad in hot water.* This was true of all the self-care activities I tried. *I was sad in bed, now I'm sad taking a walk.* I was being crushed by existential dread at home, now I'm being crushed by existential dread at the nail salon.

TMS - Out of all the alternatives to prescription drugs, this is the one that's worth a damn. In fact, I'll just write a whole chapter on my love for TMS.

SEVENTEEN

Transcranial Magnetic Stimulation

I first read about TMS because an acquaintance told me about a woman she knew who had a brain implant. The implant stimulated the part of her brain that would improve her mood. She had a remote control to "turn it on" whenever she needed. I believe she was talking about Vagus Nerve Stimulation and the description wasn't completely accurate, but it didn't matter because when I started googling "brain implant for depression," I found TMS, which is not a brain implant at all.

It stands for Transcranial Magnetic

Stimulation. A procedure that points an electromagnet at your head and sends pulses to stimulate the part of the brain that is underactive in depressed people AND helps with an array of other disorders AND has no side effects AND works for the majority of people who try it?!

Sounds like bullshit!

But I didn't mind it sounding like bullshit. I think I have proven that I would have tried almost anything.

When I told my husband, he thought it sounded like pseudoscience crap, not to be discouraging, but probably trying to protect me from false hope. The more I read about it, the more sure I was that I needed to try it. The comedian, Neal Brennan, even described TMS on a podcast and comedians are experts about being depressed. Thanks, Neal!

So where was I going to get this treatment? Let me just type it here in Goog-

THE PSYCHIATRIST THAT I CURRENTLY SEE OFFERS THIS TREATMENT AND I HAD NO IDEA. In just the other room in the same building where I was already curling up on the couch and describing my woes, there were people getting the ennui blasted out of their brains. I asked my psychiatrist why they hadn't recommended it. Turns out it was because the primary reason why I came to them was for ADHD.

Fair enough. I didn't realize my ADHD wasn't exactly ADHD, but more of a symptom of my depression. I couldn't follow simple directions. I couldn't drive and talk at the same time. I couldn't read. The ADHD drugs had me oscillating between focus and misery. They weren't working out. Can I have TMS now, please?

YES. This is my turning point, friends. That year, 2018, I was the lowest I had ever been in my life and in a few months I would be at my peak!

I chronicled my experience with TMS for *YouTube*. At the beginning of the first video, I am thin, tired, empty. After weeks of treatment, you can see a clear transformation and by the end of the same video I'm bright, calm, at peace. My fire is re-lit.

Allow me to offer more of a description. TMS is a treatment you receive every weekday for six weeks or more. Each treatment is about 20 minutes. They start off by finding the right spot on your head. They do this by measuring your head or by estimating the location with the electromagnet and zapping you until they see your thumb twitch. When they zap the place where your thumb twitches, they have a relative point to proceed from to find the right spot. They position you in a chair with a head rest, press a flat plate against the side of your head and more zapping begins.

I shouldn't say zaps, though. It feels more like an insistent finger tapping on your head. It's completely painless, but a little annoying.

The taps come in bursts followed by short breaks and while you're receiving the treatment, you watch *The Great British Bake Off* or something non-stressful. This is how I finally finished watching the series *The Office* and honestly, the part where Jim and Pam were having problems was bullshit. You know why it was bullshit? It was realistic. I don't watch *The Office* for realism. I watch it for Kevin falling down with a pot of chili.

TMS doesn't work instantly. It's gradual and has its own peaks and valleys. Here's a chart that shows the improvement on my mood based on the PHQ-9 quiz- a 9 question quiz that assigns a rating to the severity of one's depression. I started at 23 and dropped to 1.

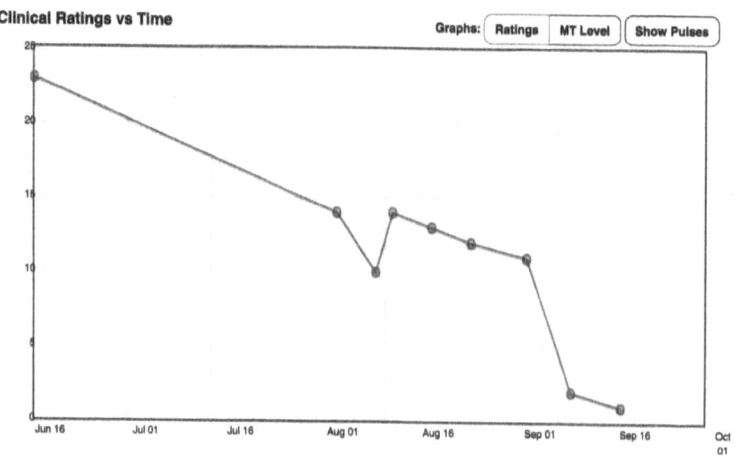

Going to a twenty minute treatment twenty minutes away from your house thirty-sixty times is tedious. I tried to make the most of it by walking on the nearby beach of the Willamette River afterwards or stopping by a local bakery for sweets.

I know I acknowledged my privilege in the disclaimer, but I feel I should acknowledge it again. I know not everyone can do this. I know there are depressed people working 60 hour weeks for low wages. I know there are parents with no childcare options. I know there are people without insurance. I know there are people who simply don't live anywhere near a place that offers TMS. I wish everyone had access to this and that's why I'm a TMS evangelist- so people can at least try to find out if it's possible for them and demand more availability.

Of course, I would never want someone to think that TMS is their final option. There are always more things to try.

TMS, though? TMS does it for me, even if I still have to take meds. The meds would be nothing without TMS.

Love you TMS.

SILLY DEPRESSED

EIGHTEEN

The World Doesn't End Tomorrow

Today I am 38. I had dreams of becoming a writer and here I am writing. Though I haven't ever made a significant amount of money doing it, writing still makes me feel good and maybe one day I'll write something that resonates with people. That's the goal. I grew up in a generation encouraged to chase our dreams!

People younger than me have grown up in a different world. I only ever had one active shooter drill towards the end of high school. Yesterday my 6 year old son had his first, of what I'm sure will be many. He was taught how to hide if bad guys come into his school.

SILLY DEPRESSED

As I mentioned, COVID-19 started when he was in preschool and I still mourn the loss of time where he could have been making friends, going to the museum and generally leading a carefree life.

While I shelter him from hearing about stressful world events, I know he's going to find out about them eventually. He's going to find out that climate change is marching us onwards towards more wildfires, hurricanes and droughts.

Our democracy is at a tipping point and I don't know which way it's going to tip.

In the midst of this, I have friends who find it absurd that they are still showing up for work every day. They feel like none of it matters.

I see young people on the internet saying they see no point in having aspirations or working towards anything. Some of them are working their asses off and still not making ends meet. I mean, what *is* the point?

If you're clinically depressed and already struggling, the weight of these problems feels doubled, doesn't it? An overwhelming number of things to care about with either an inability to care or a feeling of complete doom and no energy to do anything about anything.

During a low point I remember lying on the couch crying reading CNN. It was saying our nation was going to have another civil war. I believed it!

"Stop reading the news!" My mom scolded me. She was visiting so she could help take care of my household while I fell apart.

She was right. She practiced what she

preached too. I don't think she watches the news anymore. You know why?

For the most part, it doesn't help.

So here's what I do: I know just enough.

Honestly, I don't read the news regularly, but I still hear the highlights. They end up in *The Late Show* monologue; people talk about them. If something dangerous is happening in my vicinity, the city sends a safety alert to my phone. I read the news if something really big is happening. In general though, I know just enough. I don't need extra gruesome details knocking around in my head.

A while back, I heard an urgent message that we have only ten years to turn the "climate change ship" around and who knows how many years they're saying now. They're right. Climate change is a big deal. It's urgent. It's going to affect everyone, rich or poor, though the poor will feel it worse. Things need to be done and the issues that are most urgent to you might be different from the ones that seem most urgent to me.

But what can YOU really do about it or any other big world issue you worry about?

List, in practical terms, what concrete steps you can take to effect change in the world. I'll go first.

1. Vote and give money for politicians who I believe will steer us in the right direction in terms of the most urgent matters, like climate change, democracy, systemic injustice, and income inequality.
2. Write letters to politicians.

3. Even though it makes only a tiny difference, I can commit to consuming less.
4. Talk to friends and family members in a kind, respectful way about things I think are important.
5. Attend a protest if I really think it will be productive.
6. Cast positive images and ideas for the future.

Your list might be different from mine. You might have more power, different resources or different ideas. What can you actually do to help? Come back to your list when you feel overwhelmed or powerless.

OK, now I'm guessing you didn't write down that you should obsess over news, rip your hair out over ignorant people, get into fights with strangers on the internet, or worry.

Worry doesn't help. Knowing every little thing that happens in the world doesn't help. Predicting doom that may or may not happen doesn't help.

You might be super annoyed at me right now because you think the things I care about are dumb. Or maybe you think that I'm not treating things with enough seriousness.

But what can I do? I can spend my life wringing my hands until I die, or I can make the most of my life. I can manage my mental illness, fill my life with as many positive things as possible, act on my convictions when it's time to act, play board games with my family, and otherwise write and draw to my heart's content.

I have no idea what kind of world my son is

going to grow up in, but if and when he comes to me wondering what the point of carrying on is, here is what I will tell him: The world isn't ending tomorrow. You have time to live a meaningful life. What do you want to do? What do you want to become? There's time to do it. And although the world might be changing quite a bit, it happens slowly. I have every confidence that for the next hundred years, the world will still have use for scientists, health professionals, artists, and bakers. *Whatever* it is you want to do, there's still time to do it!

If you're asking yourself *Why do I bother showing up for school or work every day?* Maybe it's because you just kind of hate your job or feel like you're not doing something that "makes a difference." Make a plan to go in a direction that will satisfy you. And it doesn't have to be regarding your career. Maybe the thing that makes you feel like you're "making a difference" is picking up litter, gardening, being a loving parent, or riding a bike.

I know some days it's going to feel silly. There are days where the sky glows orange and ash falls and yet, here we are washing the same dish for the thousandth time, having a pitch meeting to advertise Doritos or playing a stupid sport you suck at in phys. ed. You might be 50 and still living with a roommate because Jeff Bezos spent the money that should have gone into your pocket on a rocket that looks like a suppository. In my opinion, it's OK to laugh at the ludicrousness of it all.

Laugh and then decide what you're going to

do as you carry on, because the world doesn't end tomorrow.

If you're depressed, sometimes it's just kind of impossible to feel hope. In that case, let me tell you about *my* stupid hope.

NINETEEN

My Stupid Hope and Why You Should Keep Living

Trigger Warning: Mention of Self-Harm

After making some videos about TMS that received thousands of views, I received a lot of messages from desperate people. They want so badly for it to work and they feel like it's their last hope. Some, in fact, were so miserable that they were suicidal.

It's hard to think of what to say, because I can imagine some of their follow-up responses. "Your friends and family will be heartbroken." *They're better off without me.* "You'll get better." But I'm *miserable right now.* "Think of the positive impact you can have on others." *I can't. I'm done.*

So all I can say to them is, *wait and see.*

Neither of us know what is going to happen. *Wait and see.*

I've lived in misery at times and I do think a lot of life seems pointless. Even writing this book; it will probably only be read by a dozen people and be thought of by no one within a year.

After I die, within a generation, I'll never be thought of again.

Along with my triumphs, my failures will be forgotten.

Anyone I have hurt will no longer hurt.

Despite my valleys, I continue to live with hope that I'll feel better.

And I've always been right!

Every time I've been down, I've come back up again.

I think I might as well stick around to see how life plays out. Here are some things I'm curious to see:

Robots! All kinds of robots, including the creepy ones that look like dogs.

Space, UFOs, and extraterrestrial discovery.

What my son does when he grows up.

When is everyone going to have a self-driving car? Are those bad boys gonna fly too?

Do I ever get good at drawing?

I've accepted that I will probably feel severely depressed again at some point. I plan for it. I'm ready to take it on again. I'm going to be sad in hot water, faking my way through social events, taking excessive naps so I can stop feeling, worrying about dropping a knife on the baby I don't have, and obsessing over the idea that I might projectile vomit onto a favorite writer someday.

I'm going to probably feel like I don't want to exist anymore because all my waking moments are agony.

And then one day I'll laugh at a stupid meme video. I'll put my laundry away. I'll feel like writing a new story.

Then a sense of purpose will come over me and that purpose is to tell depressed people that there's hope. Not to give up. Something is going to work. You're going to get tired, and then you're going to ask for help. And if your doctor isn't helping you, you're going to call a different one. This stuff isn't easy. Researching treatments when you can barely think and rarely stop crying isn't easy. Asking for help might not be easy either, but you're going to do it.

Some of you may still think *But not me. Nothing is working for me. Glad it worked for you, but you really don't understand.*

You're right that I don't know exactly what it's like to be you. However, call me crazy, I think you're going to find your way out the other side of this, if you try. My hope is baseless and frivolous, but I can't stop believing that *something* will work. Dare to have hope. Dare to look forward to looking forward to things again. *Wait and see.*

Now draw a picture of yourself riding this dolphin. If you're on a tablet, gently pet the dolphin and tell it "We're going to get through this, dolphin. I love you, dolphin."

APPENDIX 1
Planning a Relapse

Here is the name and number of a doctor or psychiatrist I can call:

Here are some treatments I might like to try:

Here is the name of someone trustworthy that I can tell that I'm feeling bad:

Here are some things I forget to do, but should try to do when I'm depressed:
(shower, eat meals, brush hair, etc.)

Here is a note to encourage myself to keep going:

APPENDIX 2
Talking to Your Friends and Family

Here is one possible way for you to tell someone you are depressed. Circle the appropriate responses.

For *a long time/awhile* I've known that I don't feel as good as I could. I feel a little bit *anxious/bad/sad/irritable/angry* pretty much all of the time and it's not healthy. I need help. I want to recover and actually feel happy when I'm supposed to feel happy. I really need a *doctor/counselor* and from you I need *support/rides to appointments/financial help/help with finding a practitioner/help with researching treatments*. Most of all, I need you to believe me when I say that something doesn't feel right and I need help.

When your friend/partner/parent wants to be helpful, but doesn't know how, tear out this page and hand it to them.

How to help me:
1. Don't pressure me. I know exercise is good. I know showering is good. You don't need to tell me more than once.
2. I'm not functioning at 100% right now and you won't be able to rely on me for the stuff you normally rely on me for. Right now, I just have to pare stuff down to the most important things. I'm doing everything I can to get back to 100% as soon as I can. This will take time, but it won't last forever. Please don't make me feel ashamed about the *mess/frozen dinners/inability to feel social/kids watching a bit too much TV/naps/_____*.
3. DO remind me about and help me make it to any *doctor/counseling* appointments and help me stay on track with meds. This is how I'm going to get better, but there might be times where I'm forgetful or immobilized.
4. Don't try to *fix me/be the doctor/be the counselor*. I know you. I'm sorry to tell you this, but you're not a doctor. You're a _____ You're my _____. _____, and for the love of God _____.

SILLY DEPRESSED

APPENDIX 3
Help in Difficult Moments

Panic Attacks and Depression, treatment ideas for physical symptoms:
Epsom salt bath
Herbal tea
Progressive muscle relaxation
CBD
Heavy cold pack on chest
Deep breathing
Exercise
Sunlight or Sunlamp

Panic Attacks and Depression, in-the-moment treatment ideas for mental symptoms:
Write the message your mind keeps repeating to you, then replace it with a better message.
Stupid Message: I am ugly.
Better Message: My appearance is ultimately irrelevant in terms of my happiness. I can be happy no matter what I look like.

Stupid Message: We're all gonna fuckin' die. Like, all of us. Like, soon.
Better Message: The future has some uncertainties, things will happen that are both bad and good that I don't have control over. I'm choosing hope.

Stupid Message:
Better Message:

SILLY DEPRESSED

Thank you for having this talk with me

I revealed a lot of personal, vulnerable thoughts. Why? So maybe you could feel like someone understood.

I also made a lot of dumb jokes and drew stupid pictures. Why? I don't know.

Stay well.

About the Author

Kristin Hooker is an author living in Portland, OR. She is a ghost story enthusiast and an ok roller skater. Future content can be found on Instagram @hookerthewriter, kristinhooker.com, or the Kristin Hooker YouTube Channel.

Thanks for reading!

As an independent author and publisher, I benefit greatly from positive ratings and reviews.

www.ingramcontent.com/pod-product-compliance
Lightning Source LLC
Chambersburg PA
CBHW030306100526
44590CB00012B/543